# PERFECTED PRAISE

## Leading Children
## Into Meaningful Worship

*Richard F. Malm*

**Destiny Image Publishers**
**P.O. Box 351**
**Shippensburg, PA 17257**

**"Speaking to the Purposes of God**
**for this Generation"**

ISBN 914903-62-4

For Worldwide Distribution
Printed in the U.S.A.

# Dedication

To my wife, Jana —

She brings me good ... all the days of her life.
Charm is deceptive, and beauty is fleeting;
but a woman who fears the Lord is to be praised.

# In Appreciation

To Pastor Warren J. Piersol, who launched me
into ministry and has shown me what it means to
be "a balanced man."

To Pastor Samuel Kelley, whose wise counsel and
unfaltering love have taught me to "bless 'em,
bless 'em."

# Foreword

When Moses stood before Pharaoh with the Divine commandment "Let My people go," the powerful ruler of Egypt relented slowly. Little by little he compromised with God's will, and after eight increasingly devastating plagues he offered to allow the adults to go worship the Lord, but the children were to be left behind. Moses categorically rejected this offer. He said, "We will go with our young and our old; with our sons and our daughters, with our flocks and our herds we will go, for we must hold a feast to the Lord" (Exodus 10:9). Moses well knew how short-lived the worship experience would be if the children were not taken along.

Too often the children have been ignored in the present resurgence of praise and worship. They are often shuttled off to a film or a game room somewhere on the premises while the adults enjoy their worship experience. If this continues, our revival of worship will perish with us. Just as we are indebted to the rich heritage of our past, so we are obligated to pass on to the future generation the richness we have discovered in worship. This can only be done while we yet live and while we are still associated with those who will comprise the church of tomorrow.

Worship is natural to children, unless they have been inhibited by adults. Dr. Benson, the founder of the modern Sunday school program, repeatedly declared, "It is as natural for a child to turn to God as it is for a morning glory to turn to the sun." It may be natural, but it is not necessarily inherent. Children need to see adults worshipping, and then they need to be led in worship. They need the worship experience tailored to their intellectual level and to their attention span. Few persons doubt this need, but even fewer leaders seem to know how to meet it.

If there is a current book that gives guidance in meeting this challenge I am totally unaware of it. When I read the manuscript for the book *Perfected Praise, Leading Children Into Meaningful Worship* I urged Richard Malm to print it and make it available to the Body of Christ. The principles and practical guidance that are expressed in this book will prove to be invaluable to those who seek to lead children into a vital expression of their love for Jesus. It should be a reference text for every Christian school and for every children's worker in our churches. I commend this book to pastors and parents and pray that God will use it to help all of us bring our children with us into the worship of the Lord.

Judson Cornwall

1988

# Contents

# Preface

Contained in these few pages are principles and insights that were mined and refined over a period of several years. I wish to express my appreciation to the excellent faculty and staff who served with me at Faith Christian School in Corpus Christi, Texas, during the years we were venturing into this uncharted realm. Their insights, feedback and daily labor at developing the character of Jesus in the lives of their students provided a fertile seedbed for discovering methods of nurturing the tender shoots of worship in the lives of the children.

This book could actually be considered a primer on the subject of children's worship. Much understanding regarding this topic is still in the secret realm of things belonging to God (Deuteronomy 29:29) and awaits a "king" willing to search deeper into the heart of God to bring forth the glory of His revelation for the world to see (Proverbs 25:2). I make no claim that this contains the final word on the topic and therefore I wish to invite your response to the work. Surely there are insights you have received that could further the church's understanding in this area.

As you read, I pray "that the God of our Lord Jesus Christ, the glorious Father, may give you the Spirit of wisdom and revelation, so that you may know him better. I pray also that the eyes of your heart may be enlightened in order that you may know the hope to which he has called you, the riches of his glorious inheritance in the saints, and his incomparably great power for us who believe."

Richard Malm
P.O. Box 488
Kerrville, TX 78029

May 1988

# Introduction

## The Direction of the Nation

It is easier to understand a nation by listening to its music than by learning its language. *Author unidentified*

But you are a chosen people, a royal priesthood, *a holy nation*, a people belonging to God, *that you may declare the praises of Him* who called you out of darkness into His wonderful light. (I Peter 2:9, emphasis added)

Music reflects the heart and soul of a nation. The dreams, priorities, aspirations and mores of a people create the raw material with which the musician works. The Russian composer Mikhail Glinka said it this way: "A nation creates music — the composer only arranges it." [9] A Turkish proverb says, "As the music is, so are the people of the country." [9] The psalmist declared that the joyful songs of the Lord could not be sung while

Israel was held captive in Babylon (Psalms 137). Songs of joy must be reserved for the joyful because music echoes the heart.

By listening to the music of a nation, much can be learned about the direction of that nation, and if one knows the direction of a nation, much can be determined about the destiny of that nation. Peter said the church is a select, holy nation, comprised of people from all nations. The church is a chosen people belonging to God for a specific purpose. God has chosen the church so it may declare His praises. It is a nation destined to bring praise and worship to Him, who has called it out of darkness and into light.

Recently the music of the church has reflected a move toward worship. Many noted Christian artists have shifted the focus of their ministry from entertaining songs *about* God and the Christian life to songs directed *to* God with the purpose of ministry to Him. While a large segment of contemporary Christian music still deals with entertainment, many of the established artists and leaders in the field are moving toward songs that minister to the Lord and encourage God's people to declare His praises.

Not only is praise and worship the direction for God's holy nation, the church, it is also the destiny of God's people. The book of Revelation, which unveils the destiny of the church, is a book filled with examples of praise and worship. Revelation 19 pictures the church standing before God's throne and declaring His greatness. Could it be that the current emphasis on praise and worship is designed to prepare the church for that great day? By learning to worship, God's people are rehearsing for that day when the dark glass will be removed and they will see Him face to face (I Corinthians 13:12). Worship experiences give a taste of heaven's splendor.

## Let the Little Children Come

Then Moses and Aaron were brought back to Pharaoh. "Go, worship the Lord your God," he said. "But just who will be going?"

Moses answered, "We will go with our young and old, *with our sons and daughters*, and with our flocks and herds, because we are to celebrate a festival to the Lord." (Exodus 10:8, 9, emphasis added)

While speaking to Pharaoh, Moses required that the children accompany them on their journey to worship God in the wilderness. Pharaoh agreed to let the men go but wanted to keep the children to insure the Israelites' return. Moses would not accept this compromise. God wanted the children to be a part of the worship experience.

Jesus also believed that praise should include children. When the chief priests became indignant at the jubilant worship the children expressed toward Jesus, He told them that from the lips of children and infants God ordained praise (Matthew 21:16). This was reminding them of what David said in Psalms 8:2.

As the church prepares herself to stand before the throne of God and worship His excellency, it is imperative that the children be part of the worship experience. Hear again the voice of Jesus saying, "Let the little children come to me, and do not hinder them, for the kingdom of God belongs to such as these" (Luke 18:16). Children are the church of tomorrow, but they are also part of the church today. They need not wait until they reach maturity to enjoy the fellowship and intimacy of worship. They need to be led into meaningful worship encounters today. To make worship meaningful, however, children must experience it at a level they are able to accept and understand.

In the summer of 1982, I was serving as principal of Faith Christian School in Corpus Christi, Texas. During that time I felt God directing me to lead the children of that school into the same sort of worship experience that many of their parents were enjoying. For the next three and one-half years, through prayer and error, learning and discerning, certain ideas and concepts began to surface. In this book I seek to share some of these ideas and concepts. This work can only provide a basic introduction to the topic of worship because so much is yet to be revealed and understood by the church. Because we will spend eternity enraptured with worship of the Heavenly Father, it cannot be expected that we will be able to grasp much of its magnitude in this short lifetime.

This thesis will begin by exploring the Old Testament foundation for worship and its pattern for spiritual worship. New Testament worship, which occurs at the level of man's spirit, and the New Testament concept of "God in us" will then be explored. Once this groundwork has been laid, some ideas will be presented on how this experience of worship at the spirit level, or spiritual worship, can be communicated to children.

## Worship Defined

Religion [or worship] that God our Father accepts as pure and faultless is this: to look after orphans and widows in their distress and to keep oneself from being polluted by the world. (James 1:27)

According to *Strong's Dictionary of the Greek New Testament* [12], the Greek word *threskeia* used by James in chapter 1, verse 27, above can be translated either as "religion" or as "worship." This scripture then gives a very concise definition of "pure and faultless" worship. Biblical worship is a life style of obedience to God and of service to our fellow man. An obedient and compassionate life style is the ultimate act of worship. "If you love me, you will obey what I command" (John 14:15).

Recently, however, the term "worship" has come to be associated with religious activities performed at a worship service. Bulletins list the order of "worship" and men and women serve as "worship" leaders. None of these relate to the "pure and faultless" worship that James spoke of. Actually they refer to an experience that has come to be called "worship."

These two understandings of the word "worship" are closely linked. In order to properly enter into the worship experience, a person's life style must be one of "pure and faultless" worship. A worship experience that does not spring from a life style of worship will be merely an emotional event devoid of any true spiritual significance.

This book will concentrate on how to lead children into a meaningful worship *experience* or encounter with their Heavenly Father. The basis of this worship experience will be a life of compassion and obedience. Unless both the worship leader and the worshippers are living lives of worship, all the methods and techniques discussed later will be useless emotional manipulations.

# Chapter One

# Biblical Worship

## The Old Testament Shadow

The law is only a shadow of the good things that are coming — not the realities themselves. For this reason it can never, by the same sacrifices repeated endlessly year after year, make perfect *those who draw near to worship*. (Hebrews 10:1, emphasis added)

Therefore do not let anyone judge you by what you eat or drink, or with regard to a religious festival, a New Moon celebration or a Sabbath day. These are a shadow of the things that were to come; the reality, however, is found in Christ. (Colossians 2:16, 17)

To aid His people in understanding the mysteries of the unseen spiritual realm, God has given pictures in the physical realm. For example, the spotless lamb that was acceptable as a sacrifice in Old Testament worship was a picture of Jesus, the sinless Lamb of God (John 1:29). The death of this spotless, sinless lamb atoned for the sins of the entire world (Revelation 5). The deliverance of Israel from Egyptian bondage, the crossing of the Red Sea, the wilderness wanderings, and God's physical provisions of food and water were all given as examples to the New Testament church (I Corinthians 10:1-11).

This section will begin by reviewing the physical activities involved in Old Testament worship. These activities were a shadow of the reality of worship that was to be revealed through Jesus Christ. This section will conclude by detailing the spiritual reality the Old Testament pictures portrayed.

After the nation of Israel had been born through a deliverance from the womb of Egypt, God gave Moses instructions regarding a tabernacle they were to build for Him. Moses was given very detailed directions about the building materials, furnishings, dimensions, and all aspects of this tabernacle's construction. Moses was warned by God to "make this tabernacle and all its furnishings exactly like the pattern I will show you" (Exodus 25:9, 40). According to the specifications, this tabernacle was to be divided into three areas: the courtyard, the holy place, and the holy of holies. (See illustration on next page)

The outermost area of the tabernacle was the courtyard. It was the largest area, and it was also the only section not covered by a roof. In this courtyard stood two pieces of furniture. The brazen altar, where the sacrificial lamb was slain, was located near the entrance to the courtyard. Behind the altar stood the laver, or bronze basin, where the priests were required to wash their hands and feet before entering the enclosed and covered holy places (Exodus 30:19-21).

The first covered area of the tabernacle was the holy place. On a daily basis, the priests would enter this area to perform certain prescribed functions. This holy place contained three articles of furniture. Upon entering the holy place, immediately to the priest's right was a table that held twelve cakes of bread. These cakes, or "bread of the Presence," were arranged in two stacks of six each. To the priest's left was the lamp stand, which provided the necessary light within this section of the tent. There oil-fueled lights were to be kept burning continually from evening until morning (Exodus 27:21). Directly in front of the priest when he entered the holy place stood the golden altar of incense. Twice daily, specially prepared incense was offered on this altar. Once a

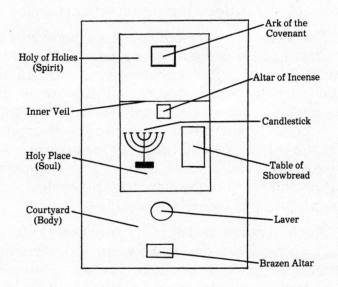

Ark of the Covenant

Holy of Holies (Spirit)

Altar of Incense

Inner Veil

Candlestick

Holy Place (Soul)

Table of Showbread

Courtyard (Body)

Laver

Brazen Altar

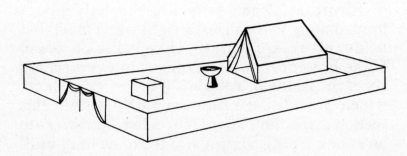

**Illustration #1**
**The Mosaic Tabernacle**

year a blood atonement was also offered on two horns that protruded from the altar (Exodus 30:10).

Attached to the holy place and separated only by a thick veil was the third area of the tabernacle, known as the holy of holies. While the priests entered the holy place on a daily basis, only one priest, once a year, was permitted to pass beyond the veil and enter the holy of holies. This most holy place was where God met the priest to accept his offering for the sins of the nation. This was the dwelling place of God, where man could meet God to worship Him. The holy of holies only contained one piece of furniture — a wooden box overlaid with pure gold, known as the Ark of the Covenant, where God said He would meet with Moses (Exodus 25:22).

Once a year, on the Day of Atonement, the high priest would cautiously enter the holy of holies with a blood sacrifice to atone for the sins of the Hebrew nation. Though the blood of an animal could never pay the price required for man's sin, God counted it as an atonement to delay the necessary judgment that accompanies sin. All of the details and ritual associated with the priestly sacrifices, priestly garments, tabernacle structure and furnishings were designed to depict or be a shadow of what God's Messiah would do in reality.

Each article and activity painted a picture of the work that Jesus would someday perform.

**The New Testament Reality**

When Christ came as high priest of the good things that are already here, he went through the greater and more perfect tabernacle that is not man-made, that is to say, not a part of this creation. He did not enter by means of the blood of goats and calves; but ... *by His own blood*, having obtained eternal redemption.... For Christ did not enter a man-made sanctuary *that was only a copy* of the true one; He entered heaven itself, now to appear for us in God's presence. (Hebrews 9:11, 12, 24, emphasis added)

Therefore, brothers, since we have confidence to enter the Most Holy Place by the blood of Jesus, by a new and living way opened for us through the curtain, that is, His body ... let us draw near to God with a sincere heart ... (Hebrews 10:19-22)

After Jesus Christ was raised from the dead He took His blood and literally presented it on an altar in heaven as the payment for man's rebellion and sin. This is seen clearly in the above passages and by applying some reasoning to some other verses. When Jesus first appeared to Mary after

His resurrection, He said, "Do not hold on to me, for I have not yet returned to the Father" (John 20:17). Once ceremonially clean and prepared to offer the blood of the sacrifice, a priest could not be touched until after completing the ceremony.

Later in the same chapter Jesus appeared and told Thomas to touch the nail holes in His hands and the hole where His side had been pierced (John 20:27). Obviously, Jesus had now returned to the Father and come back to see His disciples.

In Luke 24:39, the disciples feared that Jesus was a ghost. He said, "It is I myself! Touch me and see; a ghost does not have flesh and bones, as you see I have." His encouragement to touch Him shows that He had already been to see the Father. Then when He described His composition, He said He was flesh and bone, not flesh and blood. His blood had been presented to the Father on an altar in heaven, as a very real price paid for the very real sins of the entire world. What had been pictured by the sacrifice of an innocent lamb was now a reality through the death of the sinless Lamb of God.

The death of Christ on the cross tore back the veil that had concealed God from the average man. To graphically illustrate this new accessibility, at the very moment Jesus died, God tore the curtain in the Temple from top to bottom

(Matthew 27:51). The distinctive direction of the
tear, top to bottom, reaffirmed that the action
originated with God. Assuming a man were
capable of rending such a massive tapestry, he
would have had to tear it from bottom to top. This
destruction of the physical veil that concealed the
holy of holies was symbolic of a new bridge
established between God and man. No longer did
man need to fearfully approach God through an
earthly priest. Jesus had now opened a new and
living way to approach the Father (Hebrews
10:20).

What does all of this have to do with worship? If
worshipping God is enjoying and responding to
His presence, then one must know two things
before he can worship. In order to enjoy His
presence, a person must know where he can find
God. Where does God dwell? Once he knows
where God is, he must know how he can approach
Him. The sacrifice of Jesus answers the question
of how a person can personally find God. God is
not found through certain rituals, priestly sacrifices, or special garments. These were all pictures
of the reality found in Christ. God must be
approached through a new and living way. In
other words, God must be approached through
everyday life. There is no longer a need for a
priest to represent man before God because God
has called all to be priests unto Him (I Peter 2:9).

Man can boldly come into the presence of a holy God because the blood of God's sinless Son cleanses us from all sin and makes all who believe into sinless children of God.

This is how man is able to come before God but he must also know where he can find God. Since God no longer dwells in the holy of holies or a temple made by man, where is He?

**Where God Dwells**

Don't you know that you yourselves are God's temple and that God's Spirit lives in you? If anyone destroys God's temple, God will destroy him; for God's temple is sacred, and you are that temple. (I Corinthians 3:16)

Do you not know that your body is a temple of the Holy Spirit, who is in you, whom you have received from God? You are not your own; you were bought at a price. Therefore honor God with your body. (I Corinthians 6:19-20)

It is clear that the death and resurrection of Jesus provide access to God's presence. No longer must man worship vicariously through a priest and sacrificial offerings. Worship now is a personal experience. The above scriptures clearly show that the God who used to dwell in the tabernacle now has taken up residence in man. Through the tabernacle and temple of old, God again provided a physical picture of this spiritual mystery — God in us.

Just as the tabernacle consisted of three parts (courtyard, holy place and holy of holies), man is a tripartite being: spirit, soul and body (I Thessalonians 5:23). It is necessary to diverge here for a moment and acknowledge that many believe that man is only dual in nature and that soul and spirit are actually one. This is a legitimate belief with strong Biblical support, and the tabernacle provides insight into this discrepancy of doctrine. The holy place and the holy of holies were a part of the same room. Both shared two common walls and the same roof. It is correct to say they were distinct rooms, but it is also correct to say they were one room divided by a veil. Soul and spirit are one but can be divided by God's Word (Hebrews 4:12) and can also be spoken of as separate entities.

The courtyard was symbolic of the body. It was not covered and was open to the common man's view even as the body is the part of man exposed and visible to the world around. The soul, a more concealed and intimate part, is pictured by the holy place. The elements of the soul include the will, the intellect and the emotions. Finally, the most secluded part is man's spirit. Just as God dwelt in the holy of holies, and there chose to meet with man, today God meets with man and communes with man at the level of his spirit. This clarifies what Jesus meant when He said, "God is spirit, and His worshipers must worship in spirit and in truth" (John 4:24).

There were acts of sacrifice and worship that took place in the courtyard, and there are forms of worship our bodies can engage in. The Bible speaks of kneeling and bowing down (Psalms 95:6), shouting and singing (Psalms 66:1, 2), clapping (Psalms 47:1), lifting of hands (Psalms 63:4), dancing and playing of instruments (Psalms 150). All of these involve use of the body and are legitimate forms of courtyard praise and worship.

There were duties of worship performed in the holy place, and there are ways to worship God in the soul: the will, the intellect and the emotions of man. A well-performed rendition of the *Hallelujah Chorus* is sure to stir the *emotions* and *intellect* with *feelings* of awe and *thoughts* of God's resplendent majesty. The intellect can also worship through meditation on God's Word and His presence. These meditations may stir the emotions, resulting in an emotional involvement with worship. All of these occur because, as an act of the *will*, the worshipper chooses to worship God. These three components of the soul—intellect,

emotion and will — all work together and are able
to provide soulish worship.

Though courtyard worship (bodily worship)
and holy place worship (soulish worship) are
legitimate and necessary, God remains enthroned
in the holy of holies of man's life, his spirit.
Though bodily worship and soulish worship glorify
God, "Yet," Jesus said, "a time is coming and has
now come when the true worshipers will worship
the Father in spirit and truth, for they are the
kind of worshipers the Father seeks" (John 4:23).

To review, it has been shown that access to God
is through the finished work of Jesus. If a person
does not understand and believe this, when he
begins to draw close to God in worship he will
become conscious of his faults, shortcomings and
sin. This shifts his focus from God to his own
sinful nature and causes him to shrink back from
worship.

Once one accepts Christ's total payment for sin
and God's total forgiveness, he can "draw near to
God with a sincere heart in full assurance of faith,
having our hearts sprinkled to cleanse us from a
guilty conscience ..." (Hebrews 10:22). Then he
can believe that God accepts him and that God
will reward his seeking by revealing Himself
(Hebrews 11:6, Jeremiah 29:13).

It has also been shown that God is looking for those who will transcend bodily and soulish worship and press on to spiritual worship. Jesus said the Father is actually on the lookout for those who are willing to move into this level of worship.

## What Is Spiritual Worship?

The sacrifices of God are a broken spirit; a broken and contrite heart, O God, you will not despise. (Psalm 51:17)

Therefore, I urge you, brothers, in view of God's mercy, to offer your bodies as living sacrifices, holy and pleasing to God — which is your spiritual worship. (Romans 12:1)

Much still remains to be understood and revealed about true spiritual worship. This topic provides a new frontier for those willing to "press on to know the Lord" (Hosea 6:3). The above passages give some insight into spiritual worship.

First it is revealed that spiritual worship is, as stated earlier, dependent upon an obedient life style. The meaning of offering our bodies as a living sacrifice was explained by Paul earlier in the book of Romans.

"Do not offer the parts of your body to sin, as instruments of wickedness, but rather offer yourselves to God, as those who have been brought from death to life; and offer the parts of your body to Him as instruments of righteousness.... Just as you used to offer the parts of your body in slavery to impurity and to ever-increasing wickedness, so now offer them in slavery to righteousness leading to holiness." (Romans 6:13, 19)

Richard J. Foster, in his book *Celebration of Discipline* [6] says it this way: "If worship does not propel us into greater obedience, it has not been worship. Just as worship begins in holy expectancy it ends in holy obedience."

Second, Romans 12:1 shows that spiritual worship does not require many of the amenities typically associated with worship: beautiful music, comfortable seating, climate control, and pleasant surroundings. These things are all designed to please the body, while spiritual worship requires that the body be "sacrificed." This does not mean that worship is fostered by discomfort or unsightly surroundings. Comfort and worship are not mutually exclusive, but spiritual worship can occur regardless of the situation.

Paul and Silas worshipped God in a dark and filthy prison while their backs were raw and bleeding from a severe beating. God received and responded to their worship in a mighty way (Acts 16:25-34). The believer who has learned to go beyond the constraints of the physical body's desires is able to worship and "give thanks in all circumstances" (I Thessalonians 5:18).

Spiritual worship also needs to transcend the soul: the emotions, the will and the intellect. To transcend the will means God is worshipped because of who He is and not necessarily because the believer *wants* to worship. It is right to worship God, and therefore the believer chooses, as an act of the will, to engage in expressions of worship.

Spiritual worship also overrides the worshiper's intellect. Though he may not understand all, or any, of what is transpiring in his life, and it may seem that God has lost control of the circumstances, the spiritual worshipper trusts the truth of God's Word and praises Jesus for never leaving or forsaking him though the situation seems to declare that just the opposite is true. Finally, spiritual worship controls the emotions instead of following the lead provided by the emotions. The believer does not worship just because he feels saved or feels God's presence. These emotions or feelings are of the soul, while salvation and God's presence are spirit matters. The feelings of the soul do not always reveal what is transpiring in the spirit. This understanding brings a great freedom to the worshipper. Though he may feel tired, wretched, and disagreeable, God, who is very alive in his spirit, is unchanged and remains worthy of praise.

Because of the close relationship between body, soul and spirit, it is very natural for spiritual worship to impact the body and the soul. Worship often brings a renewal of energy to the body and provides an emotional lift for the soul. It is also true that involvement of the body and soul in worship can lead into spiritual worship. The spirit is always willing to worship, but the weakness of the flesh often hinders this expression (Mark 14:38). Activating and involving the flesh in worship then releases the spirit to worship also.

Ideally, all these components of man will participate in the worship of God. Bodily worship, soulish worship, and spiritual worship need to be viewed as three ingredients working together to fully express love to the Creator. After all, man is told to "Love the Lord your God with *all your heart* [spirit] and with *all your soul* and with *all your strength* [body]" (Deuteronomy 6:5, emphasis added).

As a person begins to worship in spirit and in the truth he now has, more truth will be revealed. "Whoever has will be given more ..." (Mark 4:25). Though this current understanding of spiritual worship is, at best, primitive, God has promised that the Holy Spirit will guide us into *all* truth.

Together, the church can follow Him, the Holy
Spirit, into the King's presence.

# Chapter Two

# Children's Worship

**From a Child's Perspective**

When I was a child, I talked like a child, I thought like a child, I reasoned like a child. When I became a man, I put childish ways behind me. (I Corinthians 13:11)

And Jesus grew in wisdom and stature, and in favor with God and men. (Luke 2:52)

Now, with this rudimentary understanding of the worship experience, how can these sublime concepts — access through Christ's blood, God in us, and spiritual worship — be translated to a child's vocabulary and level of understanding? The above scriptures show that a child talks, thinks, and reasons differently from an adult and that there is a growing in favor or understanding of God. In relating to children, it is helpful to understand some of the developmental stages through which they pass.

In general, a child's intellectual development progresses from the self-centered, magical thinking of a preschooler to concrete reasoning during elementary school years and finally to abstract reasoning as he approaches adolescence. Children are not miniature adults. They think, reason, and view the world entirely differently than adults.

The Swiss psychologist Jean Piaget [11] identified and labelled four developmental stages that correspond to a child's chronological age: the Sensori-motor Period (birth — two years), Preoperational Thought (two — seven years), Concrete Operations (seven — eleven or twelve years) and Formal Operations (beyond twelve years). It is not necessary to understand all the characteristics that Piaget and others have associated with these stages; however, a couple of the findings are useful to the children's worship leader.

At the Preoperational Thought level (kindergarten and first grade), a child is unable to distinguish fantasy from reality. For these children, believing in God is as easy as believing in Dad, Mom and an Easter Bunny. Around age seven, as the child begins to differentiate fantasy from reality, he also begins to move into the Concrete Operations stage of development. As the name implies, at this level a child thinks in concrete terms but does not deal well with abstract concepts. When a child at this developmental stage is told that Jesus is knocking at the door of his heart, he views Jesus as a literal little man who is knocking on a physical door inside his chest. Not until a child enters the Formal Operations level is he able to understand that this picture, taken from Revelation 3, speaks of God's Spirit calling to man's spirit.

A child's inability to relate to abstract ideas is of particular interest and importance when trying to lead children into an abstract experience, such as worship of an invisible yet omnipresent God. Once aware of the child's limitations, it is possible to develop strategies for communicating abstract spiritual truths in concrete terminology. Jesus himself demonstrated the best way to accomplish this transition from abstract to concrete. Repeatedly He said, "The kingdom of heaven is like ..." (Matthew 13). By comparing abstract ideas to tangible things the child has experienced, it is possible for him to grasp many spiritual truths.

Because God was diligent to provide physical illustrations of spiritual truths, it is almost always possible to find a way to help a child "see" spiritual reality. For example, in worship, Jesus is "seen" with the spiritual eyes or eyes of the heart. Closing the physical eyes helps a child's spiritual eyes see God more clearly. God is "heard" with the ears of the heart. By encouraging children to use the ears and eyes of their heart, the worship leader is able to help children relate to God communicating with them in their spirit. It is a childish understanding, but it conveys the truth in such a way that the child can expand it as his capabilities for understanding increase. More examples will be provided later in this section.

It must be remembered that worship is not dependent upon a complete intellectual understanding. The intellect is a function of the soul, while worship occurs at the level of the spirit. A child's spirit is able to comprehend ideas far beyond the child's mental abilities. Scripturally, this is illustrated when, at Mary's greeting, John the Baptist leaped for joy within his mother's womb (Luke 1:44). This had to be an outward manifestation of the joy of John's spirit because intellectually he could not possibly have recognized Mary's voice or known she was to be the mother of the Christ.

Because worship is a spirit function, it is unnecessary to get bogged down in theological explanations; nor is it necessary to get discouraged if a child who seems to be actively involved in worship pauses long enough to kick a child standing next to him. Again, children are not miniature adults, and though their spirits are capable of understanding great spiritual revelation, their bodies and souls tend to reveal their immaturity.

**Releasing Worship**

From the lips of children and infants you have ordained praise ... (Psalm 8:2; Matthew 21:16)

At that time Jesus, full of joy through the Holy Spirit, said, "I praise you, Father, Lord of heaven and earth, because you have hidden these things from the wise and learned, and revealed them to little children. Yes, Father, for this was your good pleasure." (Luke 10:21; Matthew 11:25)

It is God's good pleasure to reveal Himself and the mysteries of His kingdom to those who come to Him as children. In fact, Jesus said, "Unless you change and become like little children, you will never enter the kingdom of heaven. Therefore, whoever humbles himself like this child is the greatest in the kingdom of heaven" (Matthew 18:3, 4). Humility is necessary to be acceptable with God, and therefore God has ordained that praise should come from the lips of humble children.

A look at the Greek text of Matthew 21:16 gives

further insight. The Greek word *katartizo*, which the *New International Version* translates as "ordained," also means "to complete thoroughly." [12] The *King James Version* quotes Jesus as saying, "out of the mouth of babes and sucklings thou hast perfected praise." Not only has God decided that children should praise Him, but He has also enabled them to be perfect conductors of praise. It is as though God tells adults to look to children for examples of what praise should be. So then, praise is in the heart of a child and needs only to be released. What catalysts can the children's worship leaders use to release this praise?

### Music

Speak to one another with psalms, hymns and spiritual songs. Sing and make music in your heart to the Lord. (Ephesians 5:19)

Let the word of Christ dwell in you richly ... as you sing psalms, hymns and spiritual songs with gratitude in your hearts to God. (Colossians 3:16)

Dr. Judson Cornwall's book *Elements of Worship* [4] has an excellent chapter examining music and worship. Dr. Cornwall pointed out that "worship predates music, for Adam worshipped God in the garden of Eden, although music is not mentioned until the birth of Jubal (Genesis 4:21), and even king David kept music as subsidiary to worship.''

He also spoke of the concept of music being a vehicle that moves man into God's presence. Music and singing are not worship, but they are a means of flowing into worship. David said to enter the Temple gates with thanksgiving and enter the courts with praise, but with joyful songs to come into the Father's presence (Psalm 100). Worship requires coming into His presence, and music is a means of transport. In Paul's letters to the believers in both Ephesus and Colossae, he listed three types of songs that are to be used in worship: psalms, hymns and spiritual songs.

*Psalms*, the longest book in the Bible, was the Hebrew hymnal. To sing psalms is to sing the Word of God. Today the church is finding exciting new release in worship through the singing of God's Word as it is found in every book of the Bible. Many modern psalmists are taking God's Word and blessing the church with new choruses of praise and worship. These modern psalms, or choruses, are a great tool for drawing worship out of children.

Because the choruses are usually simple in lyrics and melody, they are readily learned by even very young children. Once learned, they allow the child to concentrate on the object of worship rather than on the medium used to elicit that worship. The simplicity and use of modern language in these choruses also allow children to relate more easily to the words and meanings being expressed. Another advantage of choruses is their freshness. Multitudes of new choruses with fresh expressions of worship are being generated weekly. There is no reason to mindlessly continue reciting words that, because of repeated use, have lost their vitality of meaning and therefore do not inspire or encourage a worship encounter.

*Hymns* are a great heritage of the church and one of its most precious treasures. Because children need a taste of this heritage, use of modern choruses should not totally replace the singing of traditional hymns. Children still need to know that "A Mighty Fortress Is Our God" and that salvation is through God's "Amazing Grace." The heritage preserved in these songs links children to the past. This exposure to the past allows them to look to the future. A sense of heritage stimulates a sense of future destiny. If children know what those who have gone before them have endured for the sake of the cross, it challenges them to continue on that same road of courage.

Use of a hymnal, however, can be counterproductive. Younger children who are still struggling to read obviously can make very little good use out of the book. Older children make good use of the hymnal, but seldom is it the use for which it was intended. Thumbing pages or staring blankly at the page tends to become the point of focus, which actually distracts from and hinders worship. A few of the true classic hymns should be repeated frequently so the children can learn the words. New hymns can be slowly introduced as the older ones are memorized.

According to Judson Cornwall,

"One of the beauties of the old hymns is that others who have come into worship experiences have set to music their vocabularies of worship, and we can sing with them and worship with their language. Frequently, their way of expression enlarges both our concept of God and our capacity to respond to God" [4].

This not only applies to old hymns but to new choruses as well. Music allows us to expand our vocabulary of, concept of, and capacity to worship.

Before moving on to spiritual songs, one caution regarding the use of music needs to be expressed. Music is possibly the most powerful form of meditation, and as such it can be of great benefit or great harm. A song can dance around a person's heart and head for hours. When this is happening, the singer is subconsciously absorbing the message

of the music. For this reason, the children's
worship leader needs to carefully screen the songs
being used. Judson Cornwall stated, "We learn
more doctrine from the hymnbook than from the
Bible, for singing is a more powerful teaching tool
than preaching" [4]. Songs used must accurately
reflect the truth of God's Word.

One of the blessings associated with many of
the choruses today is that they are taken directly
from the scriptures; learning them enables us to
meditate on God's Word. Still, a scripture presented out of context can imply a false idea.
Choruses, as well as some of the old favorite
hymns, need to be screened for accuracy of doctrine. In leading children's worship, this is even
more vital, as children are still forming their
theological concepts. The worship leader must
take reasonable steps to insure that the music
accurately conveys the true message

*Spiritual songs*, the final category Paul spoke
of, are songs that emanate from man's spirit and
not from his mind. This is seen by Paul's con-
trasting spiritual songs with songs of the mind. "I
will sing with my spirit, but I will also sing with
my mind" (I Corinthians 14:15). He went on to say
that the words of these songs are not understood
by others. "If you are praising God with your
spirit, how can one who finds himself among
those who do not understand say 'Amen' to your

thanksgiving, since *he does not know what you are saying?*" (I Corinthians 14:16, emphasis added). It is clear from reading the entire fourteenth chapter of I Corinthians that spiritual songs are sung to God (verse 2) by man's spirit (verse 14) and are not understood by others (verse 16).

But Ephesians says to speak to one another in spiritual songs (Ephesians 5:19). It would seem that this would require an interpreter, just as tongues in public meetings need to be interpreted. "If there is no interpreter, the speaker should keep quiet in the church and speak to himself and God" (I Corinthians 14:28). He also "should pray that he may interpret what he says," so his spiritual song can encourage and strengthen others (I Corinthians 14:13).

Another view of the spiritual song was presented by Judson Cornwall. He defined spiritual songs as "extemporaneously composed musical numbers expressing ecstasy" [4]. In either case, spiritual songs are the area where children can really excel in their worship expressions. Children have an innate propensity toward original expression in song. Many teachers have experienced the frustration of "The Hummer" — a child who unconsciously hums a tune during tests and quiet time. It is common for children to create tunes to accompany their play. Their lack of concern over the musical quality allows a freedom of expression seldom paralleled in adults.

This creative drive can be directed toward God by simply encouraging the children to "sing a new song unto the Lord" (Psalm 33:3; 96:1; 98:1; 149:1). Certainly there can be no song newer than that presented to God directly from the mouth and heart of a child. Children can even be encouraged to write down their original songs of praise.

As principal of a Christian school, I encouraged the children to let me hear their songs of worship. It was my privilege to sit through many one-on-one performances of these musical gifts of worship. None were masterful works of art that shook the foundations of earth, but I do believe they brought a response in heaven. I expect to find the lyrics and music of those simple love songs permanently emblazoned on the heart of Father God.

### *Mental Images*

No one has ever seen God, but God the only Son, who is at the Father's side, has made Him known. (John 1:18)

When they saw Him, they worshiped Him; but some doubted. (Matthew 28:17)

Seeing Jesus, the resurrected Christ, brought a response of worship from His early followers. Seeing Jesus will still prompt a response of worship in the hearts of His children. Encouraging children to formulate mental pictures of the God they worship is another effective tool in releasing the worship inside a child. Some, however, have challenged this idea, claiming it to be a violation of the second commandment or akin to visualization practices utilized in the occult.

According to the *King James Version*, the second commandment says, "Thou shalt not make unto thee any graven image" (Exodus 20:4). The Hebrew word *pecet* translates as "graven," which is derived from the Hebrew word meaning "to carve." In other words, man is not to carve objects of worship. This places no limitations on the use of the imagination to visualize the splendors of heaven and the risen Lord.

The Bible is careful to not give a description of the physical attributes of the man Jesus. Apparently, a description of Him in His mortality was thought unnecessary or perhaps even detrimental. However, God does provide a detailed description of the glorified Christ. In Revelation chapter 1, the apostle John painted a mental picture of Christ Jesus in His glorified form. For decades, church literature has contained pictures of Jesus during His earthly life with no Biblical basis for the artist's conception. It is time the church began "seeing" Jesus as He is today, as He is revealed in His Word.

As for similarities between "seeing" Jesus in

worship and occult practices, Satan has always tried to pervert and counterfeit what God has given to the church. In Revelation, God gives a tour of heaven. Some of the things John saw could not be passed on to the reader, but most of the vision was intended to be shared with God's people. God wanted His people to "see" Him and the dwelling place prepared for the righteous.

Bill Gothard [7] has spoken of man's mind as a picture gallery. The world fills that gallery with ungodly images. It is the believer's duty to replace those ungodly pictures with godly images. The mind is already filled with sights. The mind is picture-oriented. How marvelous to make some of these images ones that are pictures given by God Himself.

When dealing with children, it is especially needful to use mental images because of the aforementioned concrete mental orientation of children. Children *will* form mental pictures of what they think God and heaven look like. To encourage Biblical images is to help them avoid false ideas and concepts based on their own fantasy or fancy.

Revelation 4 gives insight into the appearance of heaven's throne room, the first chapter of Revelation pictures the glorified Christ, and chapter 21 describes the New Jerusalem. These pictures can stir a child's heart to a beginning appreciation for the magnitude and awesomeness of the God they serve. Combined with music during a worship time, these heavenly pictures can create a dramatic awareness of the reality of God.

To utilize this tool of mental images, have the children "turn off their outside eyes" by closing them and "turn on their inside eyes, the eyes of their heart." Now they need to see themselves standing in God's throne room as it is described. Lead the children with phrases such as, "Do you see that rainbow? [Revelation 4:3] Did you hear that thunder and see the lightning? [Revelation 4:5] Look, there is Jesus with His brilliant white hair and bright eyes [Revelation 1:14]. Now let's sing a special love song straight to Him. Did you see Him smile as we sang to Him?" [Zephaniah 3:17]

Gentle promptings such as these allow a child to experience a trip to God's own throne room. Such experiences help to remove God from the abstract realm and make Him a real friend with whom the child can talk. To lead a child on such a journey, the worship leader, like all good guides, must be familiar with the territory. The worship leader must make frequent visits and stay in tune with God's revelation through the scriptures. If the worship leader merely shares his own fantasies of heaven, he is doing little to upgrade the quality of the child's understanding. The worship leader's tour of the heavenly realms must be solidly founded on the Bible — God's revelation of Himself and of the spiritual realm.

One word of caution is in order here. In trying to communicate the personality of God the Father, it is natural to say, "He loves you just as your earthly dad does," or, "You can talk to God just as you can talk to your earthly father." The Father heart of God is a Biblical picture that must be used carefully in a perverse society. Carl Burke [3] used this approach in communicating with a ghetto child and received this response: "If He is like my father, I sure would hate Him." The word "father" drew an inappropriate mental picture for this child.

The previous two or three generations of children at least knew what a father was supposed to be because of television and its presentation of family shows. Even if their father did not match the image, and few, if any, did, television provided a model of what a father was ideally supposed to represent and how he was supposed to respond to life's situations. Today many children have absolutely no masculine image in their home. Television used to fill some of this void by providing role models of integrity that children could emulate. Today such role models are rare treasures in

American homes and nearly nonexistent on television.

The worship leader must remain in tune with the needs and viewpoints of his particular set of children so he can portray God in ways his children can relate to.

### Modeling

I have set you an example that you should do as I have done for you. (John 13:15)

Follow my example, as I follow the example of Christ. (I Corinthians 11:1)

People have always said they would rather see a sermon than hear one. Children, too, need to see sermons more than they need to hear them. The life example of the children's worship leader can be the spark that ignites the worship tinder in a child's heart. To effectively guide children into a life of worship, the leader must live a life of worship. That includes joyful participation in the worship *experience* and also a life of "pure and faultless" worship, an obedient and compassionate life style as previously mentioned (James 1:27).

Luke 6:40 says a fully trained student will be like his teacher. By worshipping half-heartedly or as a matter of ritual rather than relationship, a leader is inadvertently training the children to be the same way. "Can a blind man lead a blind man?

Will they not both fall into a pit?" (Luke 6:39).
Unless the leader has had his spiritual eyes open
to worship, he will not lead children into spiritual
worship. How can one have his spiritual eyes
opened?

The opening of the eyes to understand worship
occurs the same way the eyes were opened to
salvation. The seeker must first acknowledge a
need ("I want to be saved" — "I want to worship").
Then the person must ask to receive ("Jesus, save
me" — "Jesus, teach me to worship"). Finally, he
must believe he has received and begin walking
and growing in the knowledge of the new
relationship.

It is not necessary to understand all about God's
plan of redemption to be saved. It is as simple as
this: "If you confess with your mouth, 'Jesus is
Lord,' and believe in your heart that God raised
Him from the dead, you will be saved" (Romans
10:9). Likewise, it does not require a full understanding of worship to begin enjoying it. Once one
begins walking in the experience, he begins to
understand more of what has transpired. To
model worship, the leader needs to have experienced it.

It has been said, "You cannot lead where you do
not go and you cannot teach what you do not
know." To lead children into worship, the leader

must have a personal growing relationship with Father God. The God the leader knows is the only God he can portray to the children. Recognizing the great responsibility of the task should serve to motivate the worship leader to carefully and prayerfully approach his duties. He who teaches others will be judged more strictly (James 3:1). Great punishment is promised to anyone who causes a "little one" to stumble or sin (Matthew 18:6). Doesn't it also follow that great reward will await those who help these "little ones" to grow in a loving relationship with their Creator?

Leading children is an awesome task but one that carries exceedingly great rewards and unsurpassed returns on investments.

# Chapter Three

# Practical Steps and Tips

## Prior to Preparation

### *Cultivate a Song in Your Heart*

It cannot be overstated that a worship leader must be a man or woman who daily lives a life style of worship. One way to foster a life style of worship is to cultivate a song of praise within one's heart. The apostle Paul urged both the Ephesians and the Colossians to "make music in your heart to the Lord" (Ephesians 5:19; Colossians 3:16).

There is a tendency today to merely listen and let others do the singing. In the car, in offices, in shops and at home, radios fill the air with music produced by others. The continual drone of the radio tends to dull the senses and neutralize creativity. A giant step is taken when the believer turns off the radio and turns on the inner melodies and creativity of the spirit.

Songs of worship and praise can become a regular part of the Christian's subconscious thought patterns. This requires cultivating or some "priming of the pump." By making praise and worship songs a conscious part of each day, these songs are introduced to the subconscious, where they can take root and grow. Once this happens, the believer will find a bubbling spring of music flowing from his spirit continually.

Another key to a singing heart is revealed in Colossians 3:16. A heart full of song is the result of a heart full of gratitude. William Bay said, "A heart abounding with thanksgiving is one prepared to offer praise to God." [1] Plant seeds of gratefulness and reap a harvest of song. Daily cultivating songs of praise in one's heart is a leap toward a continual life style of worship.

### The Children Must Be Under Control

Apart from a sovereign outpouring of God's power such as demonstrated in I Samuel 19, it is impossible to lead a rowdy group of children into a worship experience. For children to learn to worship, as with other topics of instruction, discipline and control must precede learning. The leader must know that the majority of the children will respond well to directions and be cooperative. In addition, it is imperative that any who refuse to participate will at least refrain from disturbing others.

Inevitably, there will be those children who, for various reasons, refuse to participate. Worship cannot be forced upon them. They can, and probably should, be required to participate in the bodily activities (such as standing, clapping or kneeling when others are); however, worship, spirit touching Spirit, can never occur by command.

Outside the bounds of the worship time, the leader can personally minister to these children, seeking to discern any blocks that prohibit their free expression of love for God. Such informal expressions of concern can have a marked impact upon the child's level of cooperation and can frequently lead to the child accepting Christ as Savior and Lord.

Having done all this, the ultimate outcome and change of the child's heart still remains God's responsibility. Jesus promised that He would draw these children unto Himself (John 12:32). The children's worship leader can provide a proper role model and the proper environment for worship, but the alluring of the child's heart remains the joy and responsibility of the Lord.

### *Consider Learning to Play an Instrument*

Martin Luther felt music was of key importance to all ministers:

> I always loved music; whoso has skill in this art is of a good temperament, fitted for all things. We must teach music in schools; a schoolmaster ought to have skill in music, or I would not regard him; neither should we ordain young men as preachers unless they have been well exercised in music. (Martin Luther, Table Talk, DCCCXXXVIII)

An even moderately well-played instrument adds a bright dimension to group worship. Children are gracious critics and therefore provide an appreciative audience for even the most humble beginner. Personal experience has shown that within nine months a person with no prior musical skill can learn to play a guitar well enough to begin to lead worship services for children. The new richness added to the worship is well worth the time and effort invested. One needs to start today as he will never be able to learn it at a younger age.

For added excitement during the praise time, children can be encouraged to "make a joyful noise" (Psalm 95:2) through use of instruments. Tambourines, cymbals, triangles, spoons, drums, sticks and other rhythm instruments can all be employed. Such "noise" seems foreign to a Western mind's concept of praise, but it was and is right at home among Jewish worshipers. The frequent Biblical references to shouting, playing the ram's horn (shofar), clashing cymbals and other noisy activities tend to indicate that God enjoys a bit of clamor now and then.

## Preparing to Lead

### Do Prepare!

In the name of "letting the Spirit lead," some go to lead worship without spiritual or physical preparation. One has to wonder if the Spirit could not have led during the preparation as much as it is hoped He will lead during the presentation. Worship is not merely singing a number of songs that flow well together in tempo and range, nor is it merely arranging a few components into a neat, polished package.

God knows the needs of each child who will be present during the worship service. He, therefore, should be consulted as to the direction the worship time should take. This means the leader must prayerfully and meditatively prepare while allowing God to retain the right to change the course without prior notice.

Spontaneity is an important element in worship, but when dealing with children, spontaneity quickly degenerates into chaos. The children's worship leader, perhaps even more than the adult worship leader, must be prepared. Remember, if you do not have a plan, the children will.

### *Choose Music and Activities That Direct Them Toward the Goal*

Because of Judson Cornwall's succinct manner in addressing this point, please allow for a rather lengthy quotation from two of his books.

Since the Scripturally-declared purpose of gathering together is to worship, the goal of every song service should be to bring people into a worship experience. [5] We need to remind ourselves that the person who comes to church is seldom a worshipper; he is a person who needs to be changed into a worshipper. The individual who walks into the church building has his mind on natural things. His emotions are seldom stirred toward God, and very often he is actually in an emotionally low state. He has come to church to worship, but he needs something to stimulate him to worship. God used music to transform Saul (I Samuel 10:5, 6), and nothing has yet surpassed music for effectiveness in doing this. [4]

Leading people always requires beginning where the people are. The song leader must locate their present spiritual position or he will miss them entirely, for few people will run to catch up once the march has begun. In most church services, locating the level of the people will generally be easy, for people have come to church from the activities of normal life and have a very minimum of God-consciousness. The song leader might well start with a song or chorus of personal experience or testimony — one of the many "I am" or "I have" musical testimonies. This meets the people where they are and gives them something with which to identify early in the service." [5]

With children, the opening songs need to be fun songs where they can march, stomp, clap, shout and get actively involved. Often, these fun songs have little or no spiritual significance but they help to draw all the children into participation (e.g., *Father Abraham, If You're Happy and You Know It, Arky, Arky, I'm in the Lord's Army,* etc.). Meeting children where they are means jumping in with both feet, having some fun and enjoying the excitement of life and being together.

Follow fun songs with praise songs. These songs do have significant lyrics in that they are the songs we use to tell one another *about* God and who He is to us. Examples of praise songs are *God Is So Good, Every Day With Jesus, Oh, How I Love Jesus,* and *It's So Good to Be in the Arms of the Lord.*

Once established in praise, the children are ready to progress to worship songs that minister to God. From fun, to praise, to worship — the leader's goal is to be continually narrowing the children's field of vision until finally their full attention is directed toward God the Father. Sometimes the praise-to-worship transition of focus can be accomplished as simply as changing a word or two of the chorus being used (e.g., "God Is So Good" to "God, You're So Good").

Remember the goal — to rivet the children's attention upon their Heavenly Father — and then choose music and activities that bring about that ever-narrowing scope of vision.

### Be Relatively Predictable

The goal of focusing and sustaining the children's attention on God the Father is more easily attained if the leader remains rather predictable during times of worship. When children know basically what will happen next, they can remain tuned in more to the Spirit of God without being distracted by what the leader is doing. Children feel secure with schedules and routines. An orderly and rather predictable sequence to the worship service helps children relax and concentrate on the object of their worship.

### Be Creative and Use Games

Predictability does not justify dull, routine services. The opening time, or praise time, especially, should be quite fun and exciting. Games can be very useful for the opening segment.

Songs that pit the boys' volume against the girls' volume have a real value. Most every child will vigorously participate during these songs and once they have begun to sing it is natural for them to stay interested and involved after the tempo changes. As with adults, the hardest step to take in participation is the first one.

Some songs lend themselves to inter-class competition also. For example, *Ain't It Grand to be a Christian?* can be changed to *Ain't It Grand to be in First Grade?*, *Second Grade*, etc. A little God-given creativity can turn rather ordinary songs into fun tools useful in grabbing the attention of the children and drawing them into worship.

## Leading Praise

### *Relax and Enjoy Yourself*

Tension inhibits worship. Praise is a time to be released from the anxieties of everyday life while being lifted to a recognition of the victorious life Jesus has promised. Focusing on the circumstances always brings a feeling of defeat but looking to Jesus always brings assurance of His concern for us and His ability to meet our needs.

As the leader relaxes, the worshippers relax. A tense leader will produce tense followers and tension forms a barrier that restricts expressions of love. A leader who enjoys himself tells the children that worship is an enjoyable time to be anticipated. Here again, preparation is a key. A prepared leader can be a more confident, relaxed leader.

Once the worship leader has convinced the children that "it is good to praise the Lord" (Psalm 92:1), it is easy to also convince them that "it is good to be near God" (Psalm 73:28) in worship. A worship leader who enjoys praising and worshipping God will naturally produce children who take pleasure in the same.

### *Be Flexible and Sensitive*

Children are emotional creatures and the worship leader must stay in tune with the emotional climate. There will be times when it is impossible to lead the children into a meaningful worship experience. Some examples of difficult times are: right before dismissal for a long school holiday, late in the day when minds are tired and thoughts are on going home, and a day when something very exciting is planned later in the service. At times such as these it may be best to simply have a lively time of singing.

Worship cannot be forced, so be aware of the children's response and interest level. At those times when it just isn't happening, it is better to relax and enjoy singing the fun songs and perhaps moving into some upbeat praise music.

Above all else, don't sweat it or get all anxious if things are not going as planned. Worship and perspiration do not mix (Ezekiel 44:17, 18). A leader is only a leader if someone is following. When the children don't seem able to follow, it is important to be flexible enough to change the plan and take them only as far as they are willing, or able, to go.

### Begin to Flow From Song to Song

Once the song service begins to progress beyond fun songs and into praise songs, the worship leader needs to begin going from one song directly into the next one without "commercial" interruption. Traditionally, the leader stops between songs to make an announcement or say something like, "Now we are going to sing such-and-such song." Announcements are distracting once people begin to worship and statements about the next song selection are totally superfluous. If the leader simply begins to sing the next song, it is evident to all that now they are going to sing that song.

Some interjected statements and encouragements to participate are necessary during fun songs. Some comments and encouragements are initially acceptable during praise, but the further the congregation advances into praise, and ultimately worship, the less acceptable interruptions become. The goal is to take attention off the worship leader and concentrate full attention on the Heavenly Father. Comments by the worship leader draw the worshiper's attention back to that leader and dissipate worship.

The comic strip character Andy Capp made a statement that song leaders would do well to remember as worship begins. After infuriating his wife with a clever insult, Andy was thrown out of the house and into the street. Lying in the gutter, Andy said, "I am full of witty sayings that are better left unsaid."

Judson Cornwall addressed the issue in this manner: "... the leader whose goal is to bring people into the worship of God will weigh his words carefully. Many a praise service has been talked to death by an anxious song leader ... A well-prepared leader can say what needs to be said in a paragraph or less." [5]

Moving from one song directly into the next and the release it provides in worship account for much of the current popularity of choruses. These simple songs provide fresh expressions of praise but they are also easily memorized and thereby free the worshiper from the encumbrance of finding pages in a hymnal.

Eliminating distractions and pauses between songs places additional preparation responsibility on the worship leader. Music chosen must either be in the same key or accommodations must be made for the transition from one key into the next. If other musicians are involved, they, too, must be made aware of the necessary transitions. This could be accomplished by providing a written list of the planned selections. Another method, which provides more flexibility, is a system of hand signals. For example, three fingers extended downward would indicate a move to the key with three flats, or E flat. One finger pointing upward would signal a transition to the key of G, which has one sharp. Upward signals indicate sharps while downward ones indicate flats. The key of C can be signalled by curving the fingers and thumb into a C shape. This system, which is easily learned, provides a great deal of flexibility should the leader sense a need to vary the direction of the service.

As praise flows into worship, the leader and things of this earth must begin to fade from the worshipers' consciousness. The leader's attitude must be that of John the Baptist, who, when speaking of Jesus, said, "He must become greater; I must become less" (John 3:30).

## Leading Worship

### *Lead!*

Obviously, in order to lead, one must be out in front. This has both spiritual and physical connotations. To qualify as a worship *leader*, a person must be ever growing in his knowledge of worship and, more importantly, in his relationship to the object of worship. As stated earlier, spiritual worship offers new frontiers yet to be revealed to the church. A worship leader needs to be pioneering these frontiers by studying the Word, listening to the Holy Spirit and observing how God is moving in other parts of the Body of Christ — the church.

"What has God revealed to other worship leaders? How, if at all, does this revelation relate to me and my congregation?" Answers to questions such as these will allow the worship leader to also be the spiritual leader.

It is important, too, that the worship leader be a leader in the physical aspects of worship. One area where this is very important is in the giving of necessary directions. Directions such as "Let's stand together," "You may be seated as we continue to worship," or "Let's softly speak praise to Jesus" should be given loudly and distinctly. At first this seems to contradict the idea of the leader dissolving from the worshippers' consciousness. Actually, however, bold and clear leadership is an essential part of becoming less visible.

As the musical tempo lessens and as worshippers begin to settle into the comfort of the Shekinah of God, there is a natural tendency for the leader to speak more softly, sometimes to the point of mumbling. If directions are mumbled, worshipers are distracted as they try to figure out what was said and what it is they are to do.

Children also need to be reminded that someone is in control. This provides a sense of security and helps alleviate self-consciousness. If they are being asked to stand, encouraged to kneel or exhorted to speak words of praise, they need to hear clearly what it is they are to do. "If the trumpet does not sound a clear call, who will get ready for battle? So it is with you'' (I Corinthians 14:8, 9). Lead! It frees your children to concentrate on their Savior.

### Become Invisible as God Becomes Visible

As the children's field of vision narrows and as their attention begins to focus fully on the Father, there are some things the leader can do to assist the children in maintaining their attitude of worship. As already mentioned, he should limit chatter and provide distinct and succinct directions. It is also highly recommended that children be required to keep their eyes closed and hands folded during parts of the worship. Though this is not a Biblically mandated posture for worship, it has been tried and proven to be a great method for avoiding trouble.

Closing the physical eyes helps avoid distractions and also seems to help open the spiritual eyes. Children should be encouraged to see "the Lord seated on a throne, high and exalted" (Isaiah 6:1). Folding the hands, of course, helps to limit their wandering and mischief.

Jesus told His disciples to "watch and pray" (Matthew 26:41). The children's worship leader must learn to watch and praise. Little hands have a big tendency to slip apart and begin wandering. Little eyelids that usually have a hard time staying open in church just won't stay closed when they are supposed to. A stern look and quickly inserted, gentle reminder usually brings most hands and eyelids back in line. It is counterproductive to disturb the entire worship atmosphere to rebuke one or two who are not participating. Deal with problems at a later time.

### Allow Quiet Times

Once the children have entered the holy of holies — the presence of God — and their spirits are touching God's Spirit, the leader should not be afraid to allow time for silence. Cornwall said, "Cleverness is inappropriate. Talk is unnecessary. Directions for response are superfluous. Let the people worship. Silence may be threatening to the leader, but it is golden to the worshiper." [5]

Children's workers have usually been programmed to think that unless something is always happening, pandemonium is about to erupt. During quiet times of worship, something very significant is happening. The ageless spirit of the child is communicating with the Creator. The child's spirit is being strengthened as he "waits" upon the Lord (Isaiah 40:31) and, as incredible as it sounds, this is a relationship where God, too, is blessed and pleased (Psalm 69:30, 31 and Psalm 34:1).

Moments of quiet are opportune times to encourage the children to develop their spiritual ears by listening to hear if Jesus may have something to say to them. These times are also excellent opportunities to encourage soft speaking of praise, or expressing love to the Father in the children's own words. Ideally, these expressions should be vocalized because doing so incorporates the body and soul into the process. The praise is expressed through the vocal faculties and received by the auditory system of the body. The intellect component of the soul then processes the expressions and formulates new words of praise. Thus, a circle of praise is established as adoration issues from the spirit, is expressed and received by the physical body and then is processed by the soul.

During these quiet times, it is important for the leader to remain sensitive to the promptings of the Holy Spirit. It is not unusual for the Holy Spirit to direct the leader to allow children this opportunity to ask Jesus to come into their lives. It is God's goodness that draws men to repentance (Romans 2:4) and a child can easily experience this goodness and be drawn to repentance in an intense time of personal worship.

This might also be a time when some need to confess sin. The brilliance of God's glory illuminates the dark corners of the soul and convicts us of sin. These are only two of many responses that can occur when Spirit touches spirit in worship. A time of quiet allows God's Spirit freedom to speak and minister to the child's spirit.

### Remain Aware of the Time

Worship cannot be squeezed into a tight time schedule. It does not occur under pressure and so time cannot be a critical factor, but, at the same time, it is important to realize that a child's worship will usually not be sustained as long as an adult's. This does not mean it is less meaningful or less valid.

Naturally, a child's shorter attention span is partially responsible for a child's shorter worship experience. Another, and perhaps larger in-fluence, however, is related to a child's limited ability to express his emotions.

Picture a father returning home to his family after a business trip. As soon as the children see him, they delightedly rush to greet him. The eighteen-month-old stretches out his arms to be held, but as soon as Daddy picks him up and gives him a short hug, the toddler is ready to return to play. The five-year-old wants an embrace, a kiss and some verbal interaction before being con-tented. The eight-year-old desires an even length-ier greeting and exchange of ideas. An eighteen-year-old may be seeking counsel and guidance.

As a child matures, more transpires within him and this produces more ideas and emotions to be expressed as well as a greater ability to express them. Young children will quickly empty their soul before the Heavenly Father and then be ready to rush back to play. Because expressive ability varies with age, maturity and experience, it is impossible to make predictions as to how long is appropriate based upon any single factor. Other influences, such as weather conditions, time of day and emotional climate also affect the appropriate length for the worship experience. Anywhere from thirty seconds to five minutes is normal. Sensitivity to the children, experience and, mostly, common sense will dictate when to move on with the service.

## Troubleshooting

Once we have begun to apply these principles and techniques, it is valid to ask if they are working. Are the children beginning to experience intimate communion with their Heavenly Father? Is spirit touching Spirit?

Because worship is a spirit function it cannot be quantified or evaluated in physical measures. Nevertheless, it is possible for the leader to evaluate his effectiveness. When the children and the leader have worshipped God and when human spirit has touched divine Spirit, there will be a consciousness within the leader's spirit that "we have seen His glory" (John 1:14).

A believer knows when he has been born again into God's kingdom because "the Spirit Himself testifies with our spirit that we are God's children" (Romans 8:16). This "knowing" in the spirit cannot be explained by reasoning or soulish intellect. New birth transpires in man's spirit so it is man's spirit that knows it has happened. Worship also transpires in man's spirit so, naturally, man's spirit knows when it has occurred. "For who among men knows the thoughts of a [child] except the [child's] spirit within him?" (I Corinthians 2:11). But as people of understanding, we need to reach into the deep waters of the child's heart and draw out what is there (Proverbs 20:5).

Talk with the children. Ask them about their worship time. Encourage them to expect to hear from Jesus and then provide them with opportunities to express their hearts. It is too easy for us to falsely judge what is transpiring when we only look to external appearances. This was Eli's problem when he misjudged Hannah in I Samuel 1:13 and 14. Conversation with the children will reveal their spirit, "for out of the overflow of the heart the mouth speaks" (Matthew 12:34).

If conversation exposes lack of interest or involvement, some changes need to be made. Perhaps these questions will help to reveal where and what to alter.

1. Are the children born again?
   Salvation is, of course, an understood foundation and prerequisite for any worship of the true God.

2. Is there a lack of understanding?
   An uncooperative child is not necessarily obstinate or unwilling. Most children want to please but sometimes are unable to because they are unclear as to what is being asked of them. Worship can be "strange" to the uninitiated. Although one does not have to fully understand worship to experience it, even the Psalmist himself said, "Give me understanding, and I will keep your law and obey it with all my heart" (Psalm 119:34).

3. Are my expectations unrealistic?
   As discussed earlier, children are not miniature adults. It is unrealistic to expect children to respond to worship or to sustain worship as adults do. In fact, it needs to be remembered that it is in the mouths of children, not adults, that praise has been perfected. Quite often adult worship can be so unnatural that we miss true worship (worship with reality) altogether. Children feel out of place in the ethereal atmosphere we sometimes feel is necessary for worship.

When Jesus taught, it can be safely assumed that the sounds of children frequently filled the listeners' ears. The kids were welcome where Jesus was. I am convinced that if what we are doing is so spiritual that we must exclude the children so they do not disturb the atmosphere, what we are involved in is most likely carnal and soulish instead of truly spiritual.

Judson Cornwall said it this way: "Jesus made children, rather than adults, the pattern for entering into the kingdom. We're too analytical and sophisticated in our attempts at worship and we often miss worship entirely by getting caught up in new methods. Personally, I am distressed by the growing number of Christians who proclaim their actions to be worship rather than expressions of worship. Song, dance, standing, or prostration is not worship but any of it can become an expression of worship." [13]

4. Do I worship?
As mentioned above, it is possible to become so engrossed in new methods and in setting some special atmosphere for others that the worship leader fails to communicate with the Father. Remember, you cannot lead

where you do not go. If the leader does not "come before his presence with singing" (Psalm 100:2), then those following are not likely to either.

5. Do I move into praise or worship before they are ready?

Remember to meet the children where they are emotionally and mentally. Start with fun songs celebrating life, then gradually narrow their field of focus to things God has done, attributes of His character, and finally songs of worship expressed to the Father.

6. Is it "one of those days"?

Children live primarily at an emotional level. When emotions run high (they are excited and exhilarated) or when emotions run low (they are languid or lethargic), a child's soul will easily cloud and inhibit a release of spiritual worship. As adults we should be able to transcend the restrictions of our emotions but this is more difficult for children because of their strong emotional makeup. When things just don't "click," think of the priest in Ezekiel 44:17-18 who was told to "not sweat it." Have a fun time celebrating and singing. You will never succeed at forcing worship. People can only be *led* into a love relationship such as worship. They cannot be driven into it.

Through this entire analysis process, the leader should be continually asking the Lord, "... give your servant a discerning heart to govern your people and to distinguish between right and wrong" (I Kings 3:9). Remember, it is the Father who seeks spiritual worshipers (John 4:23). Surely He will delight to give insight and answers to those who desire to worship Him in the way that He seeks.

# Chapter Four

# Especially for Parents

## The Whole Duty of Parents

Now all has been heard; here is the conclusion of the matter: Fear God and keep his commandments, for this is the whole duty of man. (Ecclesiastes 12:13)

Religion that God our Father accepts as pure and faultless is this: to look after orphans and widows in their distress and to keep oneself from being polluted by the world. (James 1:27)

My command is this: Love each other as I have loved you. (John 15:12)

Note the parallel between the "whole duty of man" given in Ecclesiastes and "pure and

faultless" religion (worship), the compassionate
life style, based on James 1:27. Fear of the Lord
will lead to keeping oneself from being polluted
by the world. Keeping His commandment of love
will lead to a compassionate life style (caring for
orphans and widows). Perhaps we could say the
whole duty of parents is to train our children to
fear God with an appropriate reverence and to
have compassion on those in need. Without these
attributes manifesting themselves in our lives, we
only deceive ourselves to say we worship. The
apostle John said that the love of God is not even
in us (I John 3:17) and both Jesus and Isaiah said
that our worship is in vain (Isaiah 29:13; Matthew
15:8, 9).

Perhaps I Corinthians 13:1-4 could be rewritten
to read:

If I worship with the finest choruses of men
and even harmonize with the angelic hosts as
I sing in the spirit, but have not love, I am only
a resounding gong or a clanging cymbal. If I
frequently flow in a prophetic song of the
Lord and can fathom all the mysteries and
beauty associated with worship in the holy of
holies, and if my worship can drive back the
vilest demons and melt the hardest hearts,
but I have not love, my worship amounts to
nothing. If I do all the worshipful things, say

all the worshipful words, sing all the worshipful songs and offer my body as a yielded
worshipful instrument, but have not love, I
gain *nothing.*

Pure and faultless worship is patient, is
kind. It does not envy, it does not boast, it is
not proud, etc.

In describing worship and the Christian life,
someone has said, "It doesn't matter how high
you jump, but how straight you walk when you
hit the ground." God forbid that we should teach
children how to "jump" without teaching them
how to "walk." It is essential we train the next
generation to worship God by being "kind and
compassionate to one another, forgiving each
other ... [being] imitators of God ... as dearly loved
children and live a life of love ..." (Ephesians 4:32-
5:2). This does not come naturally for any of us —
children or adults.

We all enter the world with clenched fists and
totally self-centered. Earl Jabay described this
situation in his book *The Kingdom of Self.* [8] "The
first thing a baby does when he comes into the
world is to establish his kingdom. He, of course, is
the king. Each time the king cries out, he is
obeyed. Roughly nine times each day he tests the
authority of his kingdom, and each time he is
gratified with the results. All he has to do is cry,

and someone will come running to attend his needs. Obviously, he is the center of the world. The world exists for him. He is a god!" At first this may seem to be a rather cynical view of the "innocence of childhood" but it illustrates that children do not "go bad" somewhere along the line. We all start out, like our father Adam, competing to be God. A primary task of parents is to train children to "come off their throne" and become conscious of and compassionate toward others. Jesus set the perfect example for this: "being in very nature God, [he] did not consider equality with God something to be grasped, but *made himself nothing*, taking the very nature of a servant, being made in human likeness ... he humbled himself and became obedient to death — even death on a cross!" (Philippians 2:6-8, emphasis added).

Maturity is that process of turning our focus of concern and compassion *outward* toward others. Christian maturity (and true spiritual worship) is the process of turning our focus of concern and passion *upward* toward God and then becoming an extension of His concern and compassion outward. If we refuse to turn our thoughts and compassions outward to encompass others we will find ourselves tormented in a hell of self-concern and self-pity. The degree to which we are able to serve others is the degree to which we find

ourselves loosed from the bondage of self. Likewise, the degree to which we are able to focus our
concerns upward toward God and His kingdom is
the degree to which we find ourselves loosed from
the bondage of this world.

We could say, then, that even a child can
measure his own level of spiritual growth and
maturity by answering this simple question:
"Whom are you thinking about?" If you are
thinking only of yourself then you are acting like a
baby. If you are thinking of others first you are
being grown-up. If you are thinking of Jesus and
His kingdom first you are being mature. A worshipful life style of compassion and obedience begins
with loving God and extends to loving your
neighbor as yourself. Father in heaven, help us as
parents to live lives of selflessness and to transmit
this same attitude to the next generation.

If I carefully consider others, God will
consider me, and in some way or other He
will recompense me. Let me consider the
poor, and the Lord will consider me. Let
me look after little children, and the Lord
will treat me as His child. Let me feed His
flock, and He will make a watered garden
of my soul. This is the Lord's own promise;
be it mine to fulfill the condition, and
then to expect its fulfillment.

I may care about myself till I grow morbid; I may watch over my own feelings till I feel nothing; I may lament my own weaknesses till I grow almost too weak to lament. It will be far more profitable for me to become unselfish, and out of love to my Lord Jesus begin to care for the souls of those around me.

C.H. Spurgeon

## Be Not Weary in Well-Doing

Not that I have already obtained all this, or have already been made perfect, but I press on to take hold of that for which Christ Jesus took hold of me. Brothers, I do not consider myself yet to have taken hold of it. But one thing I do: Forgetting what is behind and straining toward what is ahead, I press on toward the goal to win the prize for which God has called me heavenward in Christ Jesus. (Philippians 3:12-14)

And Jesus grew in wisdom and stature, and in favor with God and men. (Luke 2:52)

Trust in the Lord with all your heart and lean not on your own understanding; in all your ways acknowledge him, and he will make your paths straight. (Proverbs 3:5, 6)

Parenting is undoubtedly one of the most demanding ministries to which a person can be

called. It entails long hours and thousands of
judgment calls where only God knows if you did
the right thing, at the right time, in the right way,
to the right one with the right mixture of firmness
and grace. In this abyss of uncertainty it is quite
normal for the conscientious parent to feel like a
total failure.

These feelings of defeat are made more acute if
we compare our children to others. Books such as
this can inadvertently add to our discouragement
by implying that if you do these things your
children will immediately flourish spiritually and
become little Davids or Samuels. We tend to
forget that we only see "snapshots," brief glimpses,
of other children, but living with our own gives us
the full moving picture complete with sound
effects. Need we become discouraged if spiritual
progress seems slow, or nonexistent, in our children's lives? As always, scripture provides insight
and answers for us.

Luke 2:52 says, "Jesus grew ... in favor with
God ..." How could the holy Son of God, the
"perfect" child, *grow* in favor with God? The
word translated "favor" in this verse is the Greek
word *charis*, which means "grace." Strong's Greek
dictionary amplifies this definition by saying it is
"the divine influence upon the heart and its
reflection in the life."

In other words, even Jesus grew in the influence God had on His heart and in the way that influence reflected out through His life. Did Jesus give His parents fits? Of course He did! If you doubt that, place yourself in Mary and Joseph's sandals when their twelve-year-old son decides to stay behind in Jerusalem without telling anyone (Luke 2).

Second, the book of Genesis reveals that no child has ever been born into a perfect family. Adam and Eve probably came as close as any to being perfect parents and yet one of their boys murdered the other. If our children's salvation hinges on our being perfect parents, they are doomed for eternity. It is God's grace alone that saves, not proper child training.

This point was driven home to me when, in my first few years as principal of a Christian school, I was grappling with the question of expelling a student who had far exceeded all reasonable bounds. In conferring with the teacher I asked, "What chance does he have if we, a Christian school, give up on him?" The teacher spoke the word of the Lord when she responded, "The same chance he has always had. That child's hope has always been in Jesus Christ, never in what we could do for him." Our hope must be "built on nothing less than Jesus' blood and righteousness." [14]

God could have given us "practice kids" to learn on. Once we were proficient at parenting He could have then given us the real thing to train properly. He also could have done several other things that would have made us less dependent upon Him for daily survival. He chose not to. He wants us aware of our weakness. In fact, He wants me to "boast all the more gladly about my weaknesses, so that Christ's power may rest on me.... For when I am weak, then I am strong" (II Corinthians 12:9, 10).

Certainly we are to do what we can to influence our children toward a compassionate and obedient life style. We plant the Word of God in their lives. We take them to visit the elderly and shut-ins. We try to involve them in ministry and stimulate them to service but, in the final analysis, we must never forget that it is the *charis*, the favor, the grace of God, that draws them to His pierced side.

Pray for your children. Seek counsel and prayer support from godly parents who have raised godly children (and grandchildren). Never give up! Never quit! "Press on toward the goal." But never *trust* in your efforts. Your children are God's "workmanship" (Ephesians 2:10). Trust Him to make them into masterpieces and resist the temptation to judge the artist's work before He has completed it.

I am not what I ought to be.
I am not what I hope to be.
But, blessed be God, I am not what I was,
and by His grace I am what I am.

John Newton ...

former slave ship captain turned preacher
and author of *Amazing Grace*

**Final Words**

Someone has said, "The wisdom of the ages is to find where God is going, and go with Him." Today, God is moving His people into restored understandings of the worship experience. Jesus is preparing His bride for the glorious day when she stands before Him and the veil is removed. Worship experiences here prepare the church for that ultimate worship encounter when the beloved stands face to face with the lover. In many ways, the most intimate relationship of marriage is a picture of Christ and His church communing in worship. "For this reason a man will leave his father and mother and be united to his wife, and the two will become one flesh. This is a profound mystery — but I am talking about Christ and the church" (Ephesians 5:31, 32).

In this book I have sought to articulate some of the current understandings God is revealing to the church regarding worship. One major danger is inherent in any such work. Dissection of a living creature usually means the end of that creature's life. True worship, as any love relationship, is alive. To try and dissect it and carefully scrutinize it can put an end to its vitality and reality. Like a husband and wife's love relationship, worship cannot follow strict routines and schedules and still remain vital. As R. J. Foster warned us, "We can use all the right techniques and methods, we can have the best possible liturgy, but we have not worshipped the Lord until Spirit touches spirit." [6]

God is calling His people to allow their spirits to touch His Spirit in an intimate way. Wisdom demands we cease asking God to bless what we are doing and begin to do what God is blessing. Today, God is blessing those who are seeking to worship Him in spirit and truth.

Worship brings man into the most intimate of relationships with his Creator. Worship allows man to know God, not just know about Him. Those who know about God can tell others about God. Those who know God can make Him known, and in so doing they will cause others to thirst to know Him as well. "Oh, that we might know the Lord! Let us press on to know him, and he will respond to us as surely as the coming of dawn or the rain of early spring" (Hosea 6:3 Living Bible).

## Workshop Tape Available

Since 1984, Richard Malm has presented a one-hour workshop based upon the material in this book. The workshop includes a demonstration and a "learn-by-doing" section, both of which have proven to be helpful in clarifying some concepts presented here. Cassette tapes are available of this workshop by calling or writing:

PERFECTED PRAISE
P.O. Box 488
Kerrville, TX 78029
(512) 257-8122

## The "Doulos" Missionary Training Center

Nestled in the beautiful Hill Country of Texas, the "Doulos" Training Center provides young men and women both vocational skills and practical ministerial training through guided experience and practice. Students live in on-campus dormitories and "earn while they learn." Funds generated by student work projects help pay for their living expenses and also go to fund overseas missionary ventures where their acquired skills are put into practice. This makes the "Doulos" experience available to many students who otherwise could not afford the high costs associated with most such missionary training programs.

CALL OR WRITE TODAY FOR INFORMATION ON HOW YOU CAN BECOME A PART OF THE "DOULOS" MISSIONARY TRAINING CENTER

TRINITY WORLD OUTREACH MINISTRIES
5000 Bandera Highway
Kerrville, TX 78028
(512) 257-8122

* *Doulos* is the Greek word the apostle Paul frequently used when describing himself as a bond-servant of the Lord — a love-slave who serves his Master by choice and not by obligation.

# Bibliography

1. Bay, William. *The Beauty of Worship*. (Pacific, MO: Mel Bay Publications, Inc., 1984).

2. Blackwell, Muriel, and Rives, Elsie. *Teaching Children in Sunday School*. (Nashville, TN: Convention Press, 1976.)

3. Burke, Carl. *God Is for Real, Man*. (New York, NY: Association Press, 1966).

4. Cornwall, Judson. *Elements of Worship*. (South Plainfield, NJ: Bridge Publishing, Inc., 1985.)

5. _____ . *Let Us Worship*. (South Plainfield, NJ: Bridge Publishing, Inc., 1983.)

6. Foster, Richard J. *Celebration of Discipline*. (San Francisco, CA: Harper and Row, Publishers, 1978.)

7. Gothard, Bill. Institute in Basic Youth Conflicts. (Oak Brook, IL)

8. Jabay, Earl. *The Kingdom of Self*. (Plainfield, NJ: Logos International, 1974.)

9. Mencken, H.L. *A New Dictionary of Quotations*. (New York, NY: Alfred Knopf Publishers, 1942.)

10. Price, B. Max. *Understanding Today's Children*. (Nashville, TN: Convention Press, 1969.)

11. Smith, Marjorie. *Understanding Children*. (Nashville, TN: Convention Press, 1969.)

12. Strong, James. *A Concise Dictionary of the Words in the Hebrew Bible and the Greek Testament*. (Grand Rapids, MI: MacDonald Publishing Company, —.)

13. Quoted from a personal letter to the author, February 1987.

14. The Solid Rock. Words by Edward Mote, music by William B. Bradbury.

15. All Scripture quotations are taken from *The Holy Bible, New International Version*. (Grand Rapids, MI: Zondervan Bible Publishers, 1978.)

# PERFECTED PRAISE
## P.O. Box 488
### Kerrville, TX 78029

TO ORDER BY MAIL

Name _____

Address _____

City _____

State _____ Zip _____

Phone ( ) _____


TO ORDER BY PHONE:
CALL TODAY
1-(512)-257-8122

| QTY | ADDITIONAL BOOKS | DONATION (Includes P&H) | TOTAL |
|---|---|---|---|
| | PERFECTED PRAISE | $5.00 | |

| QTY | TAPE TITLES | DONATION (Includes P&H) | TOTAL |
|---|---|---|---|
| | * PERFECTED PRAISE | $5.00 | |
| | * DYNAMIC CHAPEL IDEAS | $5.00 | |

* Some printed material is included with each tape.   TOTAL   $

Make checks payable to: PERFECTED PRAISE

Defective items may be returned within 60 days for free replacement. All offers are subject to change. Please allow 4 weeks for delivery.

**I WOULD LIKE MORE INFORMATION ON:**

[ ]  The "Doulos" Missionary Training Program.

[ ]  Having a "Perfected Praise" Workshop presented at my church or school.

[ ]  Christian School consulting services for new or established Christian Schools.